Pictorial History Of
Lee County Schools

By
Dana Fellows

Published 2007, by Dana Fellows
Dixon IL
E-mail danafellows@yahoo.com

Visit the Lee County Genealogical Society web site at:
www.leecoilgen.org

Cover: Rachel McGaffey Fellows in front of the Sugar Grove Church and School in Palmyra Township, Lee County IL.

For all of those who had to walk to school

Pictorial History Of
Lee County Schools

By

Dana Fellows

Map of School Districts in Lee County, about 1935

Map from collection at Loveland Museum in Dixon IL

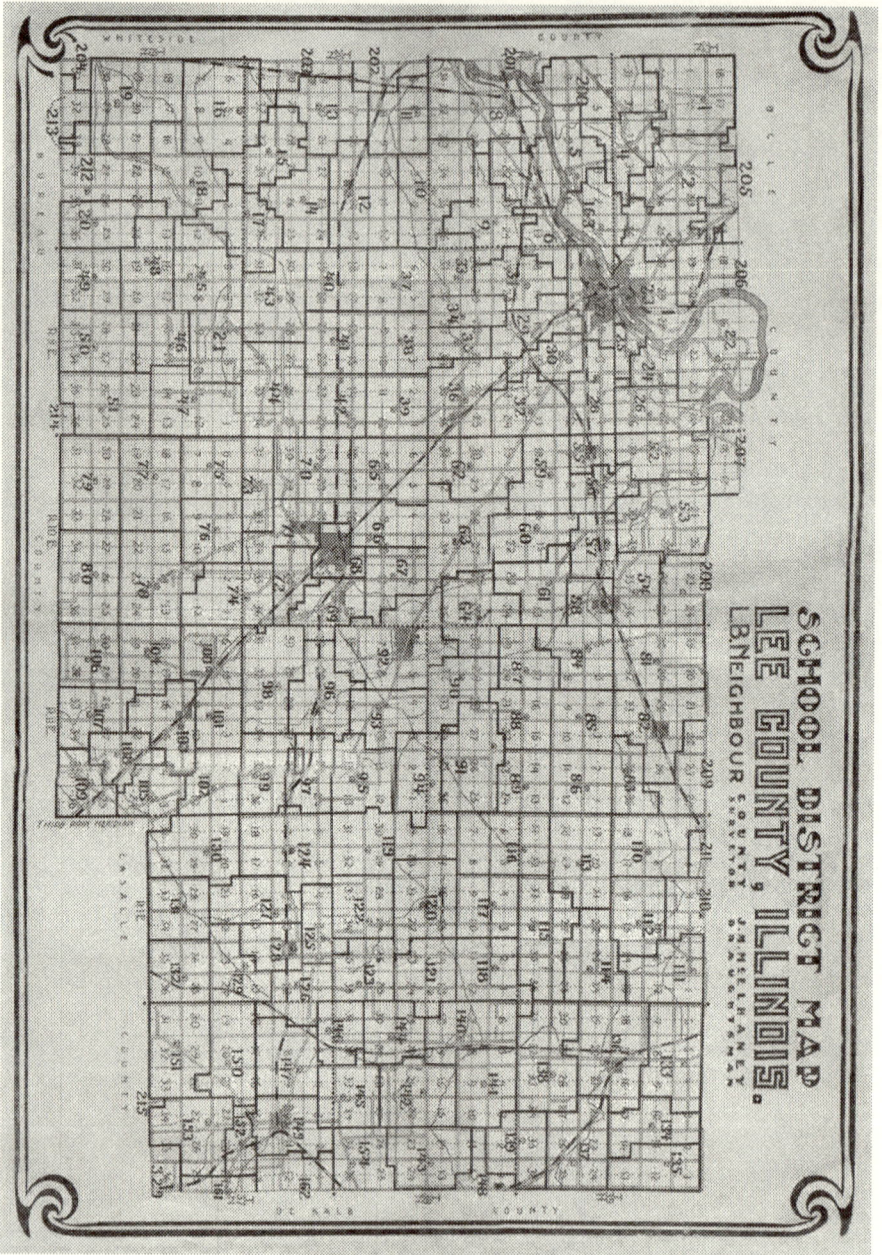

Contents

Introduction

This book was created due to a combination of factors. First I would have to go back several years ago to when I first started getting interested in local history and my family's genealogy. As I searched many of the local history books I found out that my great-great grandfather, Simon Fellows, was the first teacher in Ogle County. He taught in the 1830's at a school in Buffalo Grove, which was located west of Polo. Meanwhile, while working at the Lee/Ogle Regional Office of Education, I discovered many school pictures and records that caught my curiosity. I started to become concerned about the long term future of these pictures so I started taking them home and scanning them so that they could be preserved for future generations. Other photos were obtained from the Lee County Genealogical Society in both digital format and in documents that I scanned.

Once I had the pictures in a digital format I created a 24" by 48" poster of the schools which I labeled by district number and name. This was not meant to mean a whole lot but was rather just a small project done in my spare time. A copy of this poster hangs in the hallway of the Lee/Ogle Regional Office of Education in Grand Detour. Over the past few years the poster has stirred a lot of comments. Since doing the poster I have obtained even more pictures of old Lee County Schools.

By this time I was trying to figure out what to do with the additional photos. I thought of enlarging the poster to include the additional schools but at its already large size, I couldn't make it much bigger. The idea of putting them into a book form came to mind and that is what I decided to do. In the fall of 2006 I finally decided that I had enough to get started.

The Photo's

In 1904 the Lee County Superintendent of Schools, Isaac F. Edwards, hired a photographer to take pictures of all the school districts in Lee County. His plan was to have the photos mounted and put on display at the 1904 World's Fair in St. Louis. After the World's Fair the pictures were to be brought back to his office to be put on display. At some point the photos ended up at the Loveland Community Museum in Dixon IL. Due to the attention drawn to the pictures it was obvious that some of the schools were in poor condition. At least two of the schools, Van Campen District #122 and Foulk District #131, were rebuilt because of their appearance in the photos. The cost of building a new schoolhouse at the time was estimated at one-thousand dollars.

I tried to find at least two sources of identification for each photo but that was not always possible. The locations of the schools were found in the 1921 and 1935 Lee County Plat books. The Lee County Genealogical Society had previously identified the roads and locations of the schools which was of great assistance to me.

Some History of Lee County Schools

This book is a pictorial history and not meant to be a complete history of everything that happened at every school in Lee County. It is meant to be a collection of pictures of Lee County schools but does includes a brief history of them. There have been many history books on Lee County that are mostly narrative but do not contain any pictures of the schools. This book is intended to fill in the gap.

The first school in Lee County can be debated. I will not enter that debate but my own family history states that in 1834 Margaret Fellows, the 16 year old sister to my great-great grandfather, Simon Fellows, taught school in the home of my Fellows ancestors in Palmyra Township. In 1839 a school was built near Gap Grove and in 1841 a school was built on the John Page farm. It was there that Mary Fellows, George Page, Charles Page, Margaret Oliver, and other relatives of mine first attended school.

In 1839, about the time Lee County officially became a county, the office of Lee County Superintendent of Schools was formed. The responsibilities of the county superintendent included dispersing of funds, hiring, firing, certifying, and evaluating teachers. Keeping up with over 160 districts was an enormous task. By the time the districts started consolidating on a large scale in 1948, there were 166 school districts, 10 high school districts, one non high school district, and 143 one room schoolhouses.

In 1948 the schools in Lee County started to merge into what would be six large districts. The first was the formation of District #271 on April 17, 1948. The area included the towns of Ashton, Steward, Franklin Grove, Lee Center, Paw Paw, Compton, and West Brooklyn. On February 5, 1949, District #272 was formed and included Amboy, Eldena, Maytown, Walton, Sublette, and Harmon. Nelson Elementary District #8 remained the same and the high school students started attending Rock Falls High School. In 1956 most of the small districts near Dixon dissolved and joined Dixon District #170. On August 16, 1954, Steward detached from District #271 and formed their own elementary district and on March 16, 1956, Ashton detached and also formed their own district. About the same time, Compton and West Brooklyn detached from District #271 and joined Mendota. Several additional changes have occurred since the 1950's with the latest being in 2004 when Franklin Center detached from District #271 and joined Ashton, forming Ashton/Franklin Center Schools.

One
Alto Township

Carey School, District #133

Carey School was located on the southwest corner of Steward Road and Hayes Road in Alto Township.

Carey became part of District #271 in 1948 and was closed soon thereafter.

Finnestad School or Carlson School, District #135

Finnestad/Carlson School was located on Woodlawn Road, north of Elva Road, on the east side in Alto Township.

Finnestad/Carlson became part of District #271 on July 1, 1948 and closed in 1951.

Grimes School, District #138

Grimes school was located on McGirr Road, east of Steward Road, on north side of the road in Alto Township.

Grimes became part of District #271 in 1948. In 1954 it closed and became part of Steward, District #220.

Peterson School, District #137

Peterson School was located on the southwest corner of Reynolds and Woodlawn Roads in Alto Township. The first Peterson school was built in 1885 on ½ acre of land given by Nels Peterson that was located on his farm. The original building burned down and a new building was built in 1915. (Lee, IL - Then and Now 1874 – 1974)

Peterson School, 1915 Building

Peterson School became part of District #271 in 1948. The school closed in 1952 and was remodeled and used as a home.

After Peterson school closed, the students probably attended school in Lee, IL.

Prestegaard School, District #139

Prestegaard School was located on Herman Road, west of Woodlawn Road, on the north side of the road in Alto Township.

The Prestegaard School was built in 1865 on land that detached from the O. J. Prestegaard farm. He deeded it to the school district for as long as it was used as a school. The school closed and the students probably attended school in Lee, IL. (Lee IL - Then and Now 1874 – 1974)

In 1948 part of the Prestegaard School district annexed to District #271 and part was annexed to District #425 in Dekalb County.

The building was sold in the 1950's to Otto Oleson. In the middle of the night, sometime in 1967, an arsonist set fire to the Prestegaard School, destroying it. (Lee, IL - Then and Now 1874 – 1974)

Steward School (Built 1881), District #136

Steward School is located on the southwest corner of Perry and Steward Roads in Alto Township and in the Village of Steward.

The first school was built about 1859. Later the building was moved to the main street and was used as a store and later as a post office.

In 1881 a two story school was built at a cost of $7000. This building served the area until it was destroyed by fire in February of 1903. Classes were moved to empty store buildings and the church. Almost immediately a new school was erected in Steward. After the Steward school that was built in 1881 burned in 1903 the school board immediately approved the building of a new school. The new school was completed in November, 1903.

Steward School (Built 1881)

Steward School (Built 1903), District #136 & #252

Another school was built in 1926. The new school, built in 1926, had a much larger gymnasium. An article in the 1970 Rochelle News Leader described the gym in the old school as being so small that the free throw circles intersected with the half court jump circle. In the 1940's two, closed country schools buildings, were moved across from the existing school to provide more classroom space. They were both replaced later by two quonset huts. The school received additions in 1935 and 1962. The addition in 1962 included a music room, cafeteria, health room, class rooms and office space. The two quonset huts were removed after the additions were done. In 1998 more demolition and remodeling was done on the building.

Steward also had a High School, District #252. High school in Steward originally only consisted of two years and then later three years. The first, four-year high school class, graduated in 1932. In 1948 Steward School became part of District #271. In 1954 Steward was detached from District #271 and organized as Steward Elementary District #220. In 1955 high school students were bused to Rochelle High School.

Steward Elementary School (As of 2006)

Thorpe School, District #134

Thorpe School was located on Locust Road, north of Elva Road, on the west side of the road in Alto Township.

The school may have closed about 1945 and part of Thorpe School District became part of District #271 in 1948.

Two
Amboy Township

Amboy East Side School also known as East Frame, District #68

The 1926 Amboy High School yearbook stated that the first school in Amboy was built of logs in 1839 on the road to Sublette. In 1854 school was conducted in the old Baptist church on Mason Street and in Farwell Hall.

In 1856 a vote was taken to erect a brick building on Provost Street. Completed in 1857, this school would serve as a grade school but later high school classes were added. This school would be referred to as Old Brick after the new brick school on the west side was built in 1868. No photo could be found.

There were two other school buildings in Amboy. They were known as the East Frame (pictured above), and West Frame schools.

East Frame was originally the old Methodist Meeting House. The building was purchased about 1865 to be used as a school. In 1915 the building was renamed to Lincoln School. In 1844 East Frame School (Lincoln School) was sold at auction.

West Frame School was located near the high school that was built in 1922. The West Frame School burned down in 1923. No photo, of that school, could be located for this book.

Amboy West Brick School (Built 1868), District #68

Amboy West Brick School or also known as the Grant School was located on the northwest corner of John Street (renamed to West Provost Street in 1929) and Davis Avenue on the west side of Amboy, in Amboy Township. Amboy West Side School or Grant School was erected in 1868 and after the school was built it would be known as the New Brick School according to the 1926 Amboy Yearbook. Grant School would continue to operate until it was closed in 1922 when the new Amboy Township High School was completed. (Beckman)

Grant School as it looked in about 1926

After the Grant School was built in 1868 the four buildings were referred to as the Old Brick, New Brick, West Frame, and East Frame Buildings. These names continued to be used until the new school was built in 1896. (Beckman)

Amboy Central School, District #68

Amboy Central School was erected on Provost Street in the Town of Amboy, in Amboy Township. The school was three stories tall, including the basement, and included two gymnasiums. After Central School was built the Old Brick School Building was torn down. Central School would be used exclusively for elementary and junior high in 1922 after the new high school was built. In 1951 a new section was built in front of the original Central School. The two were connected with a passageway. The original Central School would be torn down in 1969 but the basement area would be saved and roofed to be used for storage.

In 1876 Amboy opened a high school department in the Amboy School system. Steps were taken to establish a township high school in Amboy in 1910. After a few defeats to establish a township high school from voters it finally passed in 1916. An interesting comment in the 1926 Amboy Yearbook mentioned that a passing vote in March of 1916 was voided because women were allowed to vote on the issue. Another vote was held in May of 1916 by men only and it passed. The new district would be known as Amboy Township High School District #166. District #166 opened in April 1916 and rented space at Central School District #68. In April 1920 an election was called on the proposition of building a new high school in Amboy. The proposition carried and a new high school was built in 1922. (Source: 1926 Amboy High School Yearbook)

Amboy Township High School, District #166

Amboy Township High School was located on Appleton Avenue in Amboy. Amboy Township High School started in 1916 in the Central Building and in 1922 the new school was built. When if first opened in 1922 it was not complete and work would continue on it for a few more years. (1926 Amboy High School Yearbook) In 1949 Amboy schools would consolidate and form District #272.

Current Amboy High School, District #272

In 1969 a new high school building opened, replacing the school building on Appleton Avenue, that school now houses Amboy Junior High School.

Amboy Central School (Built 1951), District #272

Amboy Central School now houses the elementary students in Amboy. Central School was used for junior high students until the new high school was built in 1969. In 1969 the junior high students moved into the high school building that was built in 1922.

Amboy Junior High School, 1958

St. Anne's School, Amboy

Located in Amboy, St. Anne's School was erected in 1923. On August 28, 1923, Sister Mary Justa with three other sisters arrived by train in Dixon having traveled from Milwaukee Wisconsin. From Dixon they traveled to the St. Anne Convent in Amboy by car. Costing forty-five thousand dollars, the school was dedicated on September 3, 1923.

The school, at one time, had almost half of the elementary students in Amboy attending it. The school suffered from low enrollment in the late 1960's and eventually closed in 1970. The building was soon sold and used for residential apartments. In 1986 the building was repurchased and is used by the church for religious educational purposes.

(Sources: Amboy – The first 150 years, 2004; St. Patrick's Church Centennial, 1857 - 1957)

Binghampton School, District #69

Binghampton School was located on Shaw Road, south of Lee Center Road, on the west side of the road in Amboy Township.

Binghampton School became part of Amboy District #272 in 1949. The school closed about 1950.

Binghampton School after the second story was removed

Elliot School, District #74

Elliot School was located on the northeast corner of Sublette and Dry Gulch Road in Amboy Township.

Elliot School became part of Amboy District #272 in 1949. The school closed about 1951.

On July 8, 1950 District #272 auctioned off Elliot School. The school was purchased by Theodore Kozak for $320. (Amboy News, July 13 1950)

The school was also known as Wheatland School. (Amboy News, July 13 1950)

Green School, District #70

Green School was located on the southwest corner of Amboy and Morgan Roads in Amboy Township.

Green School became part of Amboy District #272 in 1949. The school closed about 1952.

Holcomb School, District #73

Holcomb School was located on Morgan Road, north of Sleepy Hollow Road, on the west side of the road in Amboy Township.

Holcomb School became part of Amboy District #272 in 1949. The school closed about 1951.

On July 7, 1950 District #272 auctioned off Holcomb School. The school was purchased by Melvin Payne for $200. (Amboy News, July 13 1950)

Maine School or Welch School, District #65

Maine or Welch School was located on North Bataan Road, east of Corregidor Road, on the north side of the road in Amboy Township.

Maine or Welch School closed in 1942 and became part of Amboy District #272 in 1949.

Mynard School, District #67

Mynard School was located on Franklin Road, north of Nauman Road, on the west side of the road in Amboy Township.

Mynard School became part of Amboy District #272 in 1949. The school closed about 1949.

On July 6, 1950 District #272 auctioned off Mynard School. The school was purchased by Fred Thompson for $445. (Amboy News, July 13 1950)

Shelburn School or Rockyford School, District #71

Shelburn or Rockyford School was located on Rockyford Road, north of River View Road, in Amboy Township.

Shelburn or Rockyford School became part of Amboy District #272 in 1949. The school closed about 1949.

On July 6, 1950 District #272 auctioned off Shelburn School. The school was purchased by Harry Keyes for $1060. (Amboy News, July 13 1950)

Smith School, District #72

Smith School was located in Amboy Township.

Union Corners School, District #66

Union Corners School was located on Rockyford Road, south of Nauman Road, on the east side of the road in Amboy Township.

Union Corners School became part of Amboy District #272 in 1949. The school closed about 1949.

On July 6, 1950 District #272 auctioned off Union Corners School. The school was purchased by Bob Stewart for $600. (Amboy News, July 13 1950)

Three
Ashton Township

Drummond School or Union School, District #209

Drummond or Union School was located on the southeast corner of Gurler and Stone Roads in Ashton Township.

Drummond or Union School became part of District #271 in 1948. The school closed about 1951.

Ashton School (Built 1869), District #82

**Ashton School
1872 Lee County Plat Book**

Ashton School was located in Ashton, in Ashton Township. This school was known as Ashton Stone School and was built in 1869 with stone from the quarry at the north edge of the village. Classes at the new school started right after the New Year in January 1870. The total cost of the project was $23,000. In 1912 the school was determined to be unsafe. The cupola and its top floor were condemned. The school was closed and students attended classes in several different locations throughout the town. The school was torn down in March of 1913. (Source: Ashton Public Library)

Ashton High School (Built 1914), District #254

Ashton High School was located on the southwest corner of Route 38 and Evans Avenue in Ashton, in Ashton Township. A vote was taken and passed to construct a new school. Construction started in April, 1913 and was completed about April, 1914.

The grade school and high schools would become one district in 1939. Ashton School became part of Community Unit District #271 on July 1, 1948. Ashton District detached from District #271 on March 19, 1956 and became Ashton District #275. The building erected in 1914 was torn down in 1999.

Ashton High School in the 1940's (Built 1914)

Mills & Petrie Memorial Building

The Mills & Petrie Building was leased by the school district to be used for high school classes in the 1950's. The building's library was used for the school's study hall, social sciences and English. The building was also used for the school's cafeteria.

Ashton/Franklin Center High School (Built 1958)

In 1956 voters approved a new building to be built on Western Avenue on the west side of Ashton. Ground was broken in February of 1958 and the building was ready when classes started in August of the same year.

The 1958 building served the K-12 students in Ashton until 2004. In 2004 Franklin Center detached from District #271 and annexed to District #275. The District is now known as Ashton/Franklin Center or AFC. The building now houses the High School students from AFC.

Fell School or Beach School, District #83

Fell or Beach School was located on Beach Road, east of Ashton Road, on the south side of the road in Ashton Township.

Fell or Beach School became part of District #271 in 1948. The school closed about 1948.

Sanders School, District #81

Sanders School was located on Route 38, west of Prairie Road, on the south side of the road in Ashton Township.

Sanders School became part of District #271 in 1948. The school closed about 1955.

Four
Bradford Township

Mong School, District #84

Mong School was located near Buffalo and Reynolds Roads, on the north side of the road, in Bradford Township.

Mong School became part of District #271 in 1948. The school closed about 1949.

Mong School was also known as Dierdorff School and/or Runyan School.

Eisenberg School, District #88

Eisenberg School was located on the northwest corner Herman and Morsay Roads in Bradford Township.

Eisenberg School became part of District #271 in 1948. The school closed about 1944.

Harck School, District #90

Harck School was located on Pine Hill Road, south of Hillison Road, on the east side of the road in Bradford Township.

Harck School became part of District #271 in 1948. The school closed about 1948.

Hart School, District #87

Hart School was located on the northwest corner of Herman and Hill Roads in Bradford Township.

Hart School became part of District #271 in 1948. The school closed about 1952.

Killmer School, District #85

Killmer School was located on the southwest corner of Reynolds and Midway Roads in Bradford Township. Killmer School became part of District #271 in 1948.

The school closed in March 1956 and became part of Ashton District #275.

Vaupel School or Wellman School, District #91

Vaupel or Wellman School was located on the northwest corner of Pipeline and Ashton Roads in Bradford Township.

Vaupel or Wellman School became part of District #271 in 1948. The school closed about 1948.

Ventler School, District #94

Ventler School was located on Route 30, East of Miller Road, on the north side of the road in Bradford Township.

Ventler School became part of District #271 in 1948. The school closed about 1944.

Wagner School, District #86

Wagner School was located on the northwest corner of Reynolds and Middlebury Roads in Bradford Township.

Weishaar School, District #89

Weishaar School was located on the northeast corner of Herman and Middlebury Roads in Bradford Township.

Weishaar School closed about 1947 and in 1948, became part of District #271.

Five
Brooklyn Township

Bauer School, District #129

Bauer School was located on the northwest corner of Meridian and Meridian Roads in Brooklyn Township.

Bauer School became part of District #271 in 1948. The school closed about 1939.

Carnahan School, District #127

Carnahan School was located on the northeast corner of Route 251 and Carnahan Roads in Brooklyn Township.

Carnahan School became part of District #271 in 1948. The school closed about 1940.

Compton School, District #128

Compton School was located in the Village of Compton in Brooklyn Township. Compton School became part of District #271 in 1948. Compton annexed to Mendota in May 1954. School continued for some grades in Compton until 1966 when the Kindergarten, seventh, and eighth grade classes were sent to Mendota. (Compton Centennial Book 1875-1975)

Compton School about 1975

The following is from the Compton Centennial Book 1875 - 1975. The first school in the Compton vicinity was held in the cabin of Mr. Melugin. In 1837 the "Little Red Schoolhouse" was built. Another school house was built near the cemetery by "The Burg." In 1885 that schoolhouse was moved to the west end of Compton. This was a great feat, for all the rope in the surrounding county was collected to be used to move the school. The school was later moved again to the south side of Cherry Street. In 1895 another school was built by J. Anglemeir, which was remodeled and enlarged several times over the years. On January 10, 1928 that school was destroyed by fire. A new building was erected in 1929. At that time two years of high school was added and eventually a third. In 1949 the high school classes were dropped.

Davison School, District #126

Davison School was located on Fisk Road, north of Merriman Road, on the west side of the road in Brooklyn Township.

Davison School became part of District #271 in 1948. The school closed about 1936.

Foulk School, District #131

Foulk School was located on the northwest corner of Cottage Hill and Carnahan Roads in Brooklyn Township.

In 1904 this picture was taken to be put on a display, with the other Lee County Schools, at the St. Louis World's Fair. After seeing the condition of the school in the photograph it was decided to build a new school.

Foulk School became part of Mendota Community Consolidated District #289 in 1951. The school closed about 1945.

Kastler School, District #130

Kastler School was located on the southeast corner of Tower and Brooklyn Roads in Brooklyn Township.

Kastler School became part of Mendota Community Consolidated District #289 in 1951. The school closed about 1943.

The school's name has also been seen spelled as Kestler.

Melugin School, District #125

Melugin School was located on Shaw Road, east of Richard Road, on the north side of the road in Brooklyn Township.

The school closed about 1947 and became part of District #271 in 1948.

Politsch School, District #132

Politsch School was located on the northeast corner of Cottage Hill and Zimmerman Roads in Brooklyn Township.

Politsch School became part of District #271 in 1948. The school closed in 1949.

St. Mary's School, West Brooklyn

The construction on St. Mary's School in West Brooklyn began in the fall of 1919 and was completed in 1920. The building was dedicated on September 5th 1920 about one year after the construction had started.

The lower floor of St. Mary's School contained a Hall that could accommodate 350 people and a stage that could hold 40 people. The school's second floor had three large 20 by 26 foot classrooms with 11 foot ceilings. Stained glass and a skylight decorated the chapel in the school. Windows in the school were provided with Florentine glass which made light easy on the eyes. A modern heating system was installed in a separate building. Modern desks were installed in the school that allowed for maximum comfort for all the students. The school closed and the building was eventually torn down. Students in West Brooklyn now attend school in Mendota.

West Brooklyn School, District #124

West Brooklyn School was located on the northeast corner of Brooklyn and West Brooklyn Roads in Brooklyn Township.

West Brooklyn School became part of District #271 in 1948. West Brooklyn School District detached from District #271 and was annexed to Mendota Districts #289 and #280 April 5, 1954 by the LaSalle County Board of School Trustees. The school closed in 1954.

Six
China Township

Hausen School, District #57

Hausen School was located on Route 38, east of Rockyford Road, on the north side of the road in China Township.

Hausen School became part of District #271 on July 1, 1948. Hausen School closed in 1953.

Franklin Grove School (Built 1856), District #58

Franklin Grove School, also known as White School, was located in Franklin Grove, China Township. In the early history of the town there were a couple of different schools built. In 1856 a larger building measuring thirty feet by forty feet was built. The school had two rooms on the first floor and two on the second. In 1867 thirty feet was added to the school. High school classes were added to the upper floors. The high school drew students from many of the rural elementary schools. Soon there was a need for a larger school.

In 1894 a new school was erected in Franklin Grove. It served the needs for the elementary and high school students for many years. In the 1930's the school was becoming overcrowded. Additional classrooms were added along with indoor plumbing in 1932.

Franklin Grove School (Built 1894)

Franklin Grove School (Built 1894), District #58

Franklin Grove School (With 1937 Addition), District #58

In addition to the added classrooms and indoor plumbing being added in 1932 there was still a need for a gymnasium. A large gymnasium was built onto the school in 1937. The gym not only served the school but also served the community for other events.

On December 21, 1951 fire destroyed the school. The fire was thought to have started in the basement and spread quickly. Within minutes the entire school was engulfed in flames.

School started on time after Christmas break. Classes were held in the gymnasium where portable partitions were used to separate the classes. Some students were bused to Ashton for classes while other classes were held in church basements and other buildings in town. During basketball games the entire contents would be taken down and put back up before classes the next day. (Source: Schools of Franklin Grove by Annis Moore Spangler)

Franklin Grove Grade School (Built 1956), District #271

After the fire in 1951 one would think that a new school would immediately be built to replace the one that had burned. This would normally be true but at about this same time many changes were taking place throughout Lee County. All of the western part of Lee County was formed into one large district known as District #271. There was much debate on where and how schools were to be built. During this time Ashton and Steward both formed their own districts and Compton and West Brooklyn joined Mendota Schools. In wouldn't be until 1956 that a new school would be built. Located in the same block as the old school, dedication for the new school took place on March 18, 1956. In January of 1982 the original gym that was built in the 1930's burnt but was rebuilt and opened in 1983.

Franklin Grove High School (Built 1958), District #271

Lee Center High School students started attending classes in Franklin Grove in 1956. A new high school called Franklin Center High School was built on the east side of Franklin Grove. Construction started in 1957 and was completed in 1958. (Source: 1952 Franklin Grove and 1959 Franklin/Center Yearbooks)

Pineview School, District #54

Pineview School was located on Daysville Road, north of Mill Road, on the west side of the road in China Township.

Pineview School became part of Lee Center District #271 July 1, 1948. The school closed about 1938.

Samuel Dysart School, District #61

Samuel Dysart School was located on the southeast of corner of McGirr Road and Franklin Road in China Township.

Samuel Dysart School became part of Lee Center District #271 on July 1, 1948. On July 18, 1950, by order of the court, it once again became a district of its own. On July 16, 1956 the district dissolved and became part of District #271.

Seebach School, District #64

Seebach School was located on the northwest corner of Hillison Road and Grove Road in China Township.

Seebach School became part of District #271 on July 1, 1948. The school closed about 1951.

Sunday School, District #208

Sunday School was located on Daysville Road, north of Naylor Road, on the west side of the road in China Township.

Sunday School became part of District #271 effective July 1, 1948. Sunday School closed about 1942.

Temperance Hill School, District #63

Temperance Hill School was located on Route 52, southeast of Rockyford Road, on the south side of the road in China Township.

The Amboy News reported on August 11, 1882 that the Temperance Hill directors had decided to rebuild their recently burned down school house. The contract for the construction was awarded to C.D. Sears.

Temperance Hill School became part of Amboy District #272 effective July 1, 1949. Temperance Hill School closed about 1953.

Seven
Dixon Township

Dixon First High School, Dixon

The First High School in the City of Dixon was located at 117 East Second Street in the City of Dixon. The building was originally constructed in 1843 and used by the Methodist as their first church building. Later it was sold to the school district and became the first high school in Dixon. The basement was used for the fifth grade until the Woodworth School was built. In 1859 the school had an enrollment of 400 students and consisted of five departments. It is believed that this school served all of the needs of a high school until 1868 or 1869. (Source: Loveland Museum Records)

Other Early Dixon Schools

Stone School was built in 1847 at 212 Hennepin Avenue in the City of Dixon. In 1852 overcrowding forced some of the students to be moved to the court house. (Dixon Telegraph, February 28, 1954)

Union School was opened in 1855. In 1860 a small frame building was built next to the school to help alleviate overcrowding. In 1866 students were also being taught in the Dixon Lutheran Church. (Dixon Telegraph, February 28, 1954)

Woodworth School, District #27

Woodworth School, built in 1866, was located on the corner of Nachusa Avenue and Sixth Street in the City of Dixon, Dixon Township.

The school was originally known as the Dement Town Third Ward School but was later named Woodworth after Mrs. Woodworth. Woodworth School was closed about 1938 when Lincoln School in Dixon opened. (Dixon Evening Telegraph, February 28, 1976) The closing of Woodworth School would not be the end of the school. The building was reopened to house a private day-nursery for employees of the Green River Ordnance Plant while the plant was in operation.

In 1946 the Dixon School district was suffering overpopulation at the new Lincoln School so it was decided to reopen Woodworth to service the first, second, and third grades. (Dixon Telegraph, February 26, 1954)

Woodworth School, along with E.C. Smith School, was part of District #27 which consisted of the south side of the river in Dixon.

Red Brick School later known as E.C. Smith School, Dixon

Red Brick School, completed in 1869, was located on Seventh Street, near Highland Avenue, in the City of Dixon for a cost of $32,000. Red Brick School opened for classes in the fall of 1869. It contained eight classrooms and served the South side of Dixon. (History of Lee County, Hill Publishing, 1881) Red Brick School was also known as the Old Red Brick School and later the name was changed to E.C. Smith in honor of its former superintendent. (Stevens History of Lee County, 1914) The school operated until 1938 when Lincoln School opened and students were sent there. In the summer of 1939 the E.C. Smith School was torn down to make way for tennis courts and a playground. (Dixon Telegraph, February 26, 1954)

E.C. Smith School, along with Woodworth School, was part of District #27 which consisted of the south side of the river in Dixon.

North Dixon School, District #23

North Dixon School was located on the corner of East Morgan and Brinton Avenue. (Loveland Records) It was erected in 1868-69 at a cost of $20,000. The building was constructed of brick to the third story, with a Mansard roof, crowned with a neat belfry. Including the basement, the school was four stories high. The first two stories contained two classrooms each. The Mansard room, located on the top floor, was one large room. (History of Lee County, Hill Publishing, 1881) The school served students on the North Side of Dixon until a new High School was built next door in 1900. It then served the needs for the younger students until Washington School was built about 1954. (Source: Dixon Evening Telegraph, February 28, 1976) District #23 served the north side of the river in Dixon.

South Side School also known as White Brick School, Dixon

South Side High School, also known as White Brick School, was located on the corner of Fifth Street and Hennepin Avenue in the City of Dixon. The school was completed in 1887 and an addition was added in the winter of 1892 to accommodate more students. South Side School served both elementary and high school students until a fire destroyed the building in September 1907. (Stevens History of Lee County, 1914) White Brick School was replaced with a brand new school a few years later.

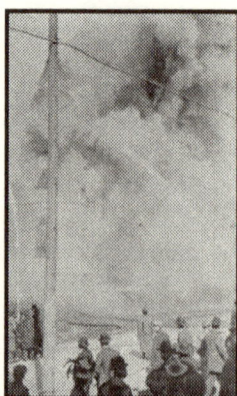

White Brick School during and after the fire in September, 1907

North Dixon High School, also known as North Side School

North Side High School was built in 1900, next to North Central School, in Dixon. North Side High School was used for high school until the new high school was built in 1929. After 1929 it was used, along with North Central School, to house elementary students until Washington School was opened in 1954. In June of 1954 the property of North Side and North Central Schools were sold at auction for $21,000 to Lowell and Olin Wilson. The North Side School was torn down and North Dixon High School would eventually be bought by St. Anne's Church to be used as a Catholic School. (Dixon Telegraph, February 26, 1954) Today Heritage Square sits on the site of the two schools.

North Dixon High and North Central Schools

Truman School, Dixon

Truman School, built in 1902, was located on the corner of West Third Street and Lincoln Avenue in the City of Dixon. The school was named after Frederick Truman who was the president of the board of education and long time mayor of the City of Dixon.

Truman School was closed when Lincoln School opened in 1938.

The building is now used for residential apartments.

South Central High School

South Central School was completed in 1908 to replace the White Brick School that burned down in 1907. Originally built as a high school it later served as an elementary school. The school is most famous for being known as the school that Ronald Reagan attended as a child. Today the building has been restored and known as the Dixon Historical Center. It is slated to open in the future as a museum displaying local history and exhibits from the Smithsonian Institute.

South Central High School in the 1950's

Loveland School, Dixon

Loveland School was located on the northwest side of Dixon on 4th Avenue, in the Swissville area. Mr. and Mrs. George C. Loveland gave $12,000 for the building of a school in 1913. Loveland School was replaced by Jefferson School

in 1954. After Loveland School was closed the building was auctioned off in June 1954. The high bid was for $5500 by Lowell and Olin Wilson, operators of Wilson Brothers Contracting. The Wilson brothers planned on building a home on the property. (Source: Dixon Telegraph, June 12, 1954)

Dixon High School, Dixon

Dixon High school is located on Peoria Avenue, in the City of Dixon. In 1918 the north and south districts were consolidated into one district and it was decided that a new, larger high school was needed. The new $600,000 High School was completed in 1929. The school replaced the North Dixon High School and the South Central High School. In 1959 two large wings and a new gymnasium were added. The gymnasium was named for a former superintendent of the school, A.H. Lancaster.

Dixon Memorial Bridge showing High School, Dixon

Lincoln Elementary School, Dixon District #170

Lincoln School is located at Lincoln Avenue and Fifth Street in the City of Dixon. Completed in 1938 for $273,000, Lincoln School replaced Woodworth School, E.C. Smith School, and Truman School. Lincoln School still operates today as an attendance center for Dixon District #170.

Lincoln Elementary School, Dixon 2006

Jefferson Elementary School, Dixon District #170

Jefferson School is located on the northwest side in the City of Dixon. Jefferson School replaced Loveland School. The cost of construction was $701,000.

On July 10, 1945, voters gave approval to purchase three parcels of land, where Washington, Jefferson, and Madison Schools were to be later located. In 1951 voters gave the okay to building Washington and Jefferson Schools. In selecting the sites, it was important to limit the amount of students travel distance to ½ mile and to eliminate the crossing of railroads and busy roads.

Jefferson School now operates as an attendance center for Dixon District #170.

Jefferson Elementary School, Dixon 2006

Washington Elementary School, Dixon District #170

Washington School is located in the City of Dixon. The cost of construction was $981,000. The building was completed about 1954.

Washington School operates as an attendance center for Dixon District #170.

Washington Elementary School, Dixon 2006

Madison School, Dixon District #170

Madison School was located in the City of Dixon. The cost of construction was $667,000. During a board meeting in 1957 the discussion of a name for the new school took place. Two names were proposed, Madison School for President James Madison and Hoover School for President Hebert Hoover. A vote was taken by the board and each name received three votes. After some consideration the Board President, John Dixon, changed his vote to Madison. His justification was that the name should be taken for one of the founding fathers of the country.

Reagan Middle School, Dixon District #170

Madison School was added onto in the early 1990's at a cost of 6.4 million dollars. The new addition added 80,000 square feet and is now called Ronald Reagan Middle School. The school houses fifth through eighth grades for Dixon District #170.

St. Mary's School

St. Mary's School was originally located at 713 South Peoria Avenue in the City of Dixon. The school was founded in 1897. (History of Lee County, Stevens)

The original St. Mary's School was in a restored house. Later a building was placed at the corner of Peoria and Seventh Street. That building was replaced with the current building pictured below. (Loveland Records)

St. Anne's School (Old North Side High School), Dixon

The old North Side High School building was purchased and used for a school until another property about ½ mile away was purchased and a new school was built there.

St. Anne's Church and School (Built 1959-60), Dixon

St. Anne's School is located on the north side in the City of Dixon. Originally the church bought the old North Central School building for the use of a school. Anticipating growth and future needs the church bought 10 acres for the purpose of building a new church and school. Construction started in October of 1959 and was completed by December of 1960. The school portion included five classrooms and a social hall. The social hall eventually became four more classrooms.

Bend School, District #22

Bend School was located on the northwest corner of Grand Detour and Sink Hollow Roads in Dixon Township.

Bend School dissolved on July 16, 1956 and became part of Dixon District #170.

The school operated as an attendance center until it closed in 1958.

Bend School 1956

Brierton School, District #24

Brierton School was located on the northeast corner of Route 2 and Sink Hollow Roads in Dixon Township.

Brierton School District dissolved on July 16, 1956 and became part of Dixon District #170.

The school operated as an attendance center for District #170 until it closed in 1957.

Brierton was once part of District #172.

Brierton School 1956

Burkett School, District #28

Burkett School was located on the southwest corner of Route 38 and Burkett Road in Dixon Township.

Burkett School closed in 1951 and dissolved on August 1, 1952. The school annexed to Garrison, Stony Point, Brierton, Nachusa, and White Temple.

Burkett School was built around 1848 and at one time was known as Gravel School. (Lee/Ogle Regional Office of Education records)

Garrison School, District #26

Garrison School was located on Maples Road, south of Naylor Road, on the west side of the road in Dixon Township.

Garrison School dissolved on July 16, 1956 and became part of Dixon District #170.

The school operated as an attendance center for District #170 until it closed in 1958.

Garrison School 1956

Hazelwood School, District #206

Hazelwood School was located on Lowell Park Road, south of Penrose Road, on the east side of the road in Dixon Township.

Hazelwood School dissolved on July 16, 1954 and became part of Dixon District #170.

Hazelwood School 1956

Stoney Point School, District #25

Stoney Point School was located on Stoney Point Road, east of Route 2, on the south side of the road in Dixon Township.

Stoney Point School 1956

Stoney Point School dissolved on July 16, 1956 and became part of Dixon District #170. The school operated as an attendance center until it closed about 1958.

Stoney Point was formerly District #172.

Stony Point School may have also been known as White Oaks School. (Lee/Ogle Regional Office of Education records)

Eight
East Grove Township

Black Oak School, District #21

Black Oak School was located west of Scout Road and south of Brewster Road in East Grove Township.

Black Oak School closed and became part of Amboy Community Unit District #272 on July 1, 1949. The students attended school at the Maytown Parish Hall beginning in 1949 and starting in 1957, at the new attendance center in Maytown.

On July 7, 1950 District #272 auctioned off Black Oak School. The school was purchased by John McCullough for $330. (Amboy News, July 13 1950)

Black Oak School may have also been known as East Grove School. (Lee/Ogle Regional Office of Education records)

Armstrong School, District #49

Armstrong School was located on the northwest corner of Pump Factory and Easy Roads in East Grove Township.

Armstrong School closed in 1950 and became part of Ohio Consolidated District #17 on September 18, 1950.

Armstrong School 1904

Davin School, District #48

Davin School was located on Maytown Road, east of Game Road, on the south side of the road in East Grove Township.

Davin School became part of Amboy Community District #272 on July 1, 1949. The school closed in 1957 and students moved to a new attendance center in Maytown.

Downey School, District #51

Downey School was located on Downey Road, south of Todd Road, on the east side of the road in East Grove Township.

Downey School closed in 1953 and dissolved in 1954.

The school was one mile north of the Bureau County line. After Downey dissolved the students attended school in Ohio. The building ended up being used as a garage in the 1970's. (Source: Ohio IL Centennial Book, 1977)

Fleming School, District #45

Fleming School was located on Pump Factory Road, south of Union Road, on the west side of the road in East Grove Township.

Fleming School closed in 1943 and became part of Amboy Community District #272 on July 1, 1949.

On July 7, 1950 District #272 auctioned off Fleming School. The school was purchased by Herman Lohse for $175. (Amboy News, July 13 1950)

Friel School also known as Hubbell, District #47

Friel School was located on Union Road, east of Scout Road, on the south side of the road in East Grove Township.

Friel School closed and became part of Amboy Community Unit District #272 on July 1, 1949. The students attended school at the Maytown Parish Hall beginning in 1949 and starting in 1957, at the new attendance center in Maytown.

On July 7, 1950 District #272 auctioned off Friel School. The school was purchased by Olen Ely for $405. (Amboy News, July 13 1950)

Friel School was also known as Hubbell School.

Murphy School, District #46

Murphy School was located on the northeast corner of Route 26 and McGinty Road in East Grove Township.

Murphy School closed in 1940. The district became part of Amboy Community District #272 on July 1, 1949.

On July 8, 1950 District #272 auctioned off Murphy School. The school was purchased by John Jacobs for $275. (Amboy News, July 13 1950)

O'Neill School, District #50

O'Neill School was located on the northeast corner of Route 26 and Easy Road in East Grove Township.

O'Neill School closed in 1949 and became part of Ohio Consolidated District #17 on July 1, 1950.

The school started in the 1860's. It was named for John O'Neill whose children attended the school. Combined with the children of the Fenwick Anderson family, it was said that they filled the school. The O'Neill School along with the Downey School and the Armstrong School became part of the Ohio District. (Source: Ohio IL Centennial Book)

Nine
Hamilton Township

Keigwin School, District #212

Keigwin School was located on Harmon Road, north of Baseline Road, on the east side of the road in Hamilton Township.

Keigwin School closed in 1924. In 1947 the District became part of Walnut Consolidated District #285.

Mekeel School, District #16

Mekeel School was located on Arch Road, west of Indian Head Road, on the south side of the road in Hamilton Township.

Mekeel School was known as District #4 prior to being District #16. (Source: Illinois Historical Society, January 1918 Issue)

Mekeel School was annexed to Walnut Community Consolidated District #285 on July 1, 1966. Mekeel School closed and was sold in 1966.

Merchant School, District #18

Merchant School was located on Harmon Road, north of McElwee Road, on the west side of the road in Hamilton Township.

Merchant School closed and was annexed to Walnut Consolidated District #285 on July 1, 1957.

Earlier Photo of Merchant School

Pope School, District #20

Pope School was located on the northeast corner of Atkinson and Easy Roads in Hamilton Township.

Pope School was annexed to Walnut Consolidated District #285 on June 28, 1952.

The original Pope School was destroyed by fire about 1916. A new school was built, which cost between $2500 and $3000. The building contained a library, reading room, and an inside toilet. The school was said to have all the luxuries of a city school. (Source: Amboy News, March 9, 1917)

Earlier Pope School Building

White Chapel School, District #19

White Chapel School was located on Keigwine Road, east of Eakle Road, on the south side of the road in Hamilton Township.

White Chapel School District dissolved and was annexed to Walnut Consolidated District #285 on July 1, 1951.

Ten
Harmon Township

Carbaugh School, District #15

Carbaugh School was located on Ryan Road, south of Dietz Road, on the west side of the road in Harmon Township.

Carbaugh School District was known as District #10 prior to being District #15. (Source: Illinois Historical Society, January 1918 Issue)

Carbaugh School District dissolved and was annexed to Walnut Consolidated District #285 in 1954.

Harmon School (Built 1900), District #12

Harmon School was located on Harmon Road, North of Sterling Road, on the east side of the road in Harmon Township.

On April 1, 1861 a new district was formed. It would be known as District #3 but would later be known as Harmon School District #12. A building fourteen by twenty feet was built and equipped for the use of a school. The building would be used as a church by the Latter Day Saints, and also for several other functions over the years.

In 1869 a new building was built north of the original building. In 1879 that building was sold. A new school was built that was later destroyed by fire. A new brick school was built in 1900. (Source: Illinois Historical Society, January 1918 Issue)

Harmon School District dissolved and was annexed to Amboy Community Unit District #272 in 1956. The school operated as an attendance center for District #272.

Kimball School, District #11

Kimball School was located on Schilpp Road, south of Route 30, on the east side of the road in Harmon Township.

Kimball School District closed and annexed to Nelson District #8 in July 1960.

Lake School, District #14

Lake School was located on Van Petten Road, east of Harmon Road, on the south side of the road in Harmon Township.

Lake School District was originally named District #1. Later several more districts would be added to Harmon Township and Lee County and Lake School District would become District #14.

The first school building in the township was built about 1857. It was described as having no doors or windows but wooden shutters were on the building to keep out rain. In 1859 the school was moved east of the highway near the railroad crossing. The school would be moved again to higher ground. In 1870 the building was sold and moved to a farm west of the village of Harmon. It is assumed that a new school was built at the site. This was referred to as the original District #1 which would later become Lake School. (Source: Illinois Historical Society, January 1918 Issue)

Lake School District dissolved July 1, 1951 and was annexed to Harmon School district #12.

Lyons School, District #17

Lyons School was located on the northwest corner of Atkinson and Arch Roads in Harmon Township.

Lyons School District included parts of old districts Union Harmon, Hamilton, East Grove, and Marion. (Source: Illinois Historical Society, January 1918 Issue)

Lyons School District dissolved and was annexed to Amboy Community Unit District #272 on July 1, 1949.

Lyons School closed in 1940. The students probably attended school in Harmon after that. On July 7, 1950 District #272 auctioned off Lyons School. The school was purchased by Charles Kerchner for $175. (Amboy News, July 13 1950)

Mannion School, District #13

Mannion School was located on Schilpp Road, north of Van Petten Road, on the west side of the road in Harmon Township.

Originally District #2 in Harmon Township, Mannion School became district #13 around 1861. (Source: Illinois Historical Society, January 1918 Issue)

Mannion School District dissolved and was annexed to Harmon School District #12 on July 1, 1951.

Eleven
Lee Center Township

Shaws School, District #96

Shaws School was located on Shaw Road, east of Inlet Road, on the south side of the road in Lee Center Township.

Shaws School District became part of Community District #271 on July 1, 1948.

Wedlock School, District #97

Wedlock School was located on Shaw Road, east of Fell Road, on the south side of the road in Lee Center Township.

Wedlock School District became part of Community District #271 on July 1, 1948. Wedlock School closed in 1945.

Black School, District #99

Black School was located north of Shady Oak Road and east of Burkhard Road in Lee Center Township.

Black School District became part of Community District #271 on July 1, 1948. Black School closed in 1936.

Ford School, District #95

Ford School was located on Schmidt Road, east of Fell Road, on the south side of the road in Lee Center Township.

Ford School District closed and became part of Community District #271 on July 1, 1948.

Ford School?

The picture on the left was identified as Ford School but I was not able to verify the identification.

Inlet School, District #93

Inlet School was located on Inlet Road, south of Dively Road, on the east side of the road in Lee Center Township.

Inlet School District became part of Community District #271 on July 1, 1948. Inlet School closed in 1949.

Above photo was taken at a later date after it had become a home.

Lee Center School (Built 1847), District #92

Lee Center School was located in the village of Lee Center, Lee Center Township.

The first school built in Lee Center was one made of logs and located by a creek. This school served the basic needs of the area for about two years until the citizens decided that a new, better school should be built. In 1839 the Lee Center Union School and Union District #1 were incorporated and a school was built. (Source: History of Lee Center Schools, Reunion Booklet, 1904 History of Lee County IL, Bardwell)

Lee Center Academy

In addition to the grade school in Lee Center there was also a school of higher learning called Lee Center Academy. In 1847 the Lee Center Academy opened for those who were interested in higher learning. The academy did very well for several years and drew professors from the East. By 1859 other schools of higher learning appeared in Amboy, Dixon, and Paw Paw. Combined with the railroad being placed to the West in Amboy the academy's enrollment declined and the building became a grade school. In 1853 a brick addition was added to the building to provide additional needed space. The building served the school until it was condemned and torn down in 1909. (Source: History of Lee Center Schools, Reunion Booklet, 1904 History of Lee County IL, Bardwell)

Lee Center School (Built 1909), District #92

In 1909 a new four room school was erected in Lee Center. Behind this building a frame building was built for the elementary students. The brick building would be destroyed by fire, burning down in 1930. Classes were held in several different buildings throughout the town until a new school was built and ready to move into a few years later. (Source: History of Lee Center Schools, Reunion Booklet, 1904 History of Lee County IL, Bardwell)

Lee Center High School, District #92 and #251

In 1935 a new school was built to replace the 1909 building. One side of the new school housed the elementary students and the other side the high school students.

Lee Center School (After Changes in 1960's), District #271

Lee Center had two separate districts up to 1948. The high school was Lee Center High School District #251 and the grade school was Lee Center Grade School District. Both became part of Community District #271 on July 1, 1948. Other schools who were part of this merger at that time were Franklin Grove, Ashton, Steward, Compton, and Paw Paw.

The district would continue to operate both the grade school and the high school until 1956. In 1957, due to enrollment dropping, Lee Center High School would merge with Franklin Grove High School to form the Franklin/Center High School.

In the early part of the 1960's the Lee Center School would undergo a major change. Several feet would be added to the front of the school changing both the size and the appearance.

The first through eighth grades would continue at the Lee Center School until 1971 when they also started attending school in Franklin Grove. In 1983 the school was closed and the rest of the grades would also be bused to Franklin Grove.

Craig School, District #98

Craig School was located on Richardson Road, east of Green Wing Road, on the north side of the road in Lee Center Township.

Craig School District became part of Community District #271 on July 1, 1948. Craig School closed in 1947.

Craig School was also known as Turner School and Ingalls School.

Twelve
Marion Township

Keefer School, District #42

Keefer School was located on Sterling Road, west of Peru Road, on the south side of the road in Marion Township.

Keefer School District became part of Amboy Community Unit District #272 on July 1, 1949. Keefer School closed in 1942 when the Green River Ordnance Plant opened up.

Leonard School, District #38

Leonard School was located on Route 26, north of Ackert Road, on the west side of the road in Marion Township.

Leonard School District became part of Amboy Community Unit District #272 on July 1, 1949. Leonard School closed in 1942 when the Green River Ordnance Plant opened up.

On July 6, 1950 District #272 auctioned off Leonard School. The school was purchased by Julia Brechon for $850. (Amboy News, July 13 1950)

McCaffrey School, District #40

McCaffrey School was located on Pump Factory Road, south of Sterling Road, on the east side of the road in Marion Township.

McCaffrey School District closed and became part of Amboy Community Unit District #272 on July 1, 1949.

On July 6, 1950 District #272 auctioned off McCaffrey School. The school was purchased by Louis Apple for $640. (Amboy News, July 13 1950)

McCaffrey School

Morrissey School, District #43

Morrissey School was located on McCoy Road, east of Pump Factory Road, on the north side of the road in Marion Township.

Morrissey School District became part of Amboy Community Unit District #272 on July 1, 1949. Morrissey School closed in 1952 and students attended school at Walton.

O'Malley School, District #39

O'Malley School was located on O'Malley Road, west of Red Brick Road, in Marion Township.

O'Malley School closed in 1942 when the Green River Ordnance Plant opened up. O'Malley School District became part of Amboy Community Unit District #272 on July 1, 1949.

Palmer School, District #41

Palmer School was located on Route 26, near Amboy Road, on the west side of the road in Marion Township. The school was located on the Wesley Palmer property.

Palmer School District became part of Amboy Community Unit District #272 on July 1, 1949. Palmer School closed in 1952 and students attended the school in Walton.

The Palmer School was moved to Amboy and is now located at the Clint Conway Historical Park. It has been remodeled in recent years and serves as a mini museum. (Source: Amboy, The first 150 Years, 2004)

Stott School, District #37

Stott School was located on Pump Factory and Rhodenbaugh Roads, on the southeast corner, in Marion Township.

Stott School District became part of Amboy Community Unit District #272 on July 1, 1949. Stott School closed in 1952 and students attended school in Walton.

Welty School, District #44

Welty School was located on McCoy Road, east of Walton Road, on the north side of the road in Marion Township.

Welty School District became part of Amboy Community Unit District #272 on July 1, 1949. Welty School closed in 1948.

On July 6, 1950 District #272 auctioned off Welty School. The school was purchased by Henry O'Hare for $495. (Amboy News, July 13 1950)

Walton School Attendance Center, District #272

After the District #271 one room schools closed in 1949, students started attending school in attendance centers. In Walton, the students attended school at the Hall. In 1958 a new attendance center was built in Walton.

Walton School closed in 1985 and now all the elementary students are bused to Central School in Amboy.

Thirteen
May Township

Avery School, District #75

Avery School was located on the southeast corner of Morgan and Briar Roads in May Township.

Avery School District closed and became part of Amboy Community Unit District #272 on July 1, 1949.

The students attended school at the Maytown Parish Hall beginning in 1949 and starting in 1957, at the new attendance center in Maytown.

On July 7, 1950 District #272 auctioned off Avery School. The school was purchased by Hazel Barnes for $335. (Source: Amboy News, July 13, 1950)

Dorsey School, District #78

Dorsey School was located on the northeast corner of Maytown and Rockyford Roads in May Township.

Dorsey School District closed and became part of Amboy Community Unit District #272 on July 1, 1949. The students attended school at the Maytown Parish Hall beginning in 1949 and starting in 1957, at the new attendance center in Maytown.

On July 8, 1950 District #272 auctioned off Dorsey School. The school was purchased by Howard Leffelman for $435. (Amboy News, July 13 1950)

Fitzpatrick School, District #79

Fitzpatrick School was located on St. Mary's Road, east of Morgan Road, on the north side of the road in May Township.

Fitzpatrick School District closed in 1948 or 49 and became part of Amboy Community Unit District #272 on July 1, 1949. The students attended school at the Maytown Parish Hall beginning in 1949 and starting in 1957, at the new attendance center in Maytown.

On July 8, 1950 District #272 auctioned off Fitzpatrick School. The school was purchased by Conrad Zimmerlein for $242.5. (Amboy News, July 13 1950)

Goy School, District #80

Goy School was located on St. Mary's Road, west of Rockyford Road, on the north side of the road in May Township.

In 1936 Goy school was completely destroyed by a fire. Snow blocked the roads and the Sublette Fire Department was not able to respond to the call. The fire was believed to have started where the furnace pipe passed through the outside wall. The contents of the school were saved and no one was injured. George Goy, who was a member of the school board, stated that the school was partially covered by insurance and was to be rebuilt in the Spring and Summer of 1937.

Goy School District closed and became part of Amboy Community Unit District #272 on July 1, 1949 The students from the Goy School District started to attend school at the Maytown Parish Hall in Maytown in 1949 and in 1957 at the new attendance center.

On July 8, 1950 District #272 auctioned off Goy School. The school was purchased by John Kessel for $1900. (Amboy News, July 13 1950)

Hall School, District #76

Hall School was located on Briar Knoll Road, east of Mazy Road, on the north side of the road in May Township.

The Amboy News reported, on November 24, 1916, that the schoolhouse in the Hall district in Maytown, about three miles south of Amboy, was burned the prior Sunday afternoon. The flames were discovered by people in the neighborhood but the fire could not be extinguished. The coal-house, situated near the school building, was also burned. The origin of the fire was unknown, but it is said that incendiarism is suspected.

Hall School District closed in 1944 and became part of Amboy Community Unit District #272 on July 1, 1949. The students would attend school at the Maytown Parish Hall starting in 1949 and then in 1957 they attended the new attendance center built in Maytown.

On July 7, 1950 District #272 auctioned off Hall School. The school was purchased by Edwin Friel for $400. (Amboy News, July 13 1950)

Loan School, District #77

Loan School was located on Maytown Road, east of Morgan Road, on the north side of the road in May Township.

John Faivre wrote about the Loan School and his experience as both a student and later as a board member. Mr. Faivre recalled that the school was in disrepair. The windows were loose and the wood on the inside walls was shrunk by the dry air. This combination made the school cold in the winter and often the students would wear their coats the whole day. In the 1930's the floor was replaced and in the 1940's he insulated the building and installed storm windows. He also bought real slate blackboards from one of the Sublette area schools and installed them in the school. (Source: John Faivre, Maytown Stories)

Loan School District #77 closed and became part of Amboy Community Unit District #272 on July 1, 1949. The students attended school at the Maytown Parish Hall and starting in 1957 at the new attendance center in Maytown.

Maytown Parish Hall, District #272

On July 1, 1949 all of the schools in May Township became part of District #272. In the summer of 1949 a deal was made with the Maytown Parish Hall to rent the building for five years for the purpose of using it as a school for grades one through eight. Movable partitions were installed to divide the interior into three classrooms. One classroom accommodated grades one and two, another grades three, four, and five and the other, grades six, seven, and eight. The advantages of closing the one room school houses and using the Parish Hall for school included a better electrical system, a better water system, inside restrooms, and efficient heat in the winter time. Movable seats were used so that the building could continue to be used for parish events. The basement was big enough to allow the children to play and kitchen facilities allowed hot lunches to be served to the children.

Maytown Attendance Center, District #272

In about 1955 voters approved a new school to be constructed in Maytown to replace the Maytown Parish Hall. The new school was completed in 1956. The new attendance center would serve the area for over the next twenty years. In August 1977 the school board voted 5-2 to close the school due to low enrollment and the high cost of operation. On July 28, 1979 the school was offered for sale by auction.

Fourteen
Nachusa Township

Dysart School also known as Collins School, District #59

Dysart School was located on the southeast corner of McGirr and Nachusa Roads in Nachusa Township.

Dysart School District closed and became part of Community District #271 on July 1, 1948. On July 18, 1950 the court ruled in favor of the district to become a common district. In 1952 the district annexed to Nachusa District #55. The building was moved to District #61 about 1952. (Lee/Ogle Regional Office of Education records)

The school was also known as Collins School and West Dysart School.

Emmett School, District #56

Emmett School was located on the northwest corner of Route 38 and Robbins Road in Nachusa Township.

Emmett School District closed in 1934 and became part of Community District #271 on July 1, 1948.

Hollister, District #62

Hollister School was located on Nachusa Road, north of South Eldena Road, on the west side of the road in Nachusa Township.

In about 1841 the first school in the area was built. Later the school was moved and was then known as "Locust Street School House." The school was moved again to the location of Hollister School. In 1925 a new building was built and the name was changed to Evergreen School. Evergreen School District became part of Amboy Community Unit District #272 on July 1, 1949. In 1957 the students from the Evergreen School started attending school in Eldena at the new attendance center. (Source: 1954 Amboy Elementary Yearbook)

Evergreen School in about 1954

Graves School, District #60

Graves School was located on Rockyford Road, south of McGirr Road, on the west side of the road in Nachusa Township.

Graves School became part of Community Unit District #271 on July 1, 1948. By order of the court the district again became a common district on July 18, 1950. In 1952 the district annexed to Samuel Dysart School District #61.

The school may have closed in 1945.

Hillside School, District #53

Hillside School was located on Naylor Road, west of Twist Road, on the north side of the road in Nachusa Township.

Hillside School District became part of Community Unit District #271 on July 1, 1948. The school stayed open until it closed in 1955.

March School, District #52

March School was located on the northeast corner of Naylor and Nachusa Roads in Nachusa Township.

March School District became part of Community Unit District #271 on July 1, 1948. March School closed in 1949.

Nachusa School, District #55

Nachusa School was located on the southwest corner of Route 38 and Nachusa Road in Nachusa Township.

Nachusa School District became part of Dixon District #170 on August 15, 1955. In 1960 the school closed and the students were transported to Dixon Schools.

Nachusa School as it looked in the 1950's

Nachusa Lutheran Home School

The Nachusa Lutheran Home has a long history of providing services to children, responding to different needs throughout it's over one hundred years of existence. Originally the home was designed to serve orphans, then eventually children who were under the care of DCFS, with the current focus of treatment for alcohol or substance addiction, or as an alternative to detainment in corrections. The school has followed the many changes as well, with different buildings and a different approach. Throughout the history of the home the Dixon Public Schools have provided educational opportunities directly or indirectly.

When the home first came into existence the children attended Lincoln School in Dixon. There are many reports of activities at Nachusa where teachers from Lincoln School attended events or activities at the home.

In 1925 the first school house was built, although records indicate that the students continued to attend the public schools mainly. This building was later used as a Chapel, and was completely destroyed by a fire in 1937.

By 1941 all children were attending public school in Dixon, in all grade levels. Eventually the population of the home changed, and many students required an intense educational approach. These services were provided by Dixon Public Schools in cooperation with the Lee County Special Education Cooperative. Students were able to attend programs at Madison School and Dixon High School, while tutoring remained in place at the Nachusa campus.

The current school building was completed in 1981, with 2 active classrooms. The building also housed the Activity Therapy department, and included a recreation center and a gymnasium. Students attended the on campus school until they were able to demonstrate the skills necessary to move to the public school setting in Dixon.

In 1986 a new program opened for students in the surrounding schools who needed the intense programming offered at the Nachusa campus, but did not require residential treatment. That school was housed in the main administration building until it became apparent that more space was needed in the school for all the students served.

About 1997, a new addition was constructed adjacent to the old school classrooms, adding 7 new classrooms and office space. This is the current existing school building. In 2000 students began receiving tutoring through the Dixon Public Schools, and in 2005 the school became an Alternative Learning Opportunity program, serving all students. The school is now an Alternative School, with two programs for residential students and one program for students who are in need of intensive services but living at home.

Contributed by Linda Delimata

Nachusa Lutheran Home School in 2007

Fifteen
Nelson Township

Cook School, District #07

Cook School 1904
Inside look at Cook school

Cook School was located on Rock Island Road, east of Harmon Road, on the north side of the road in Nelson Township.

Cook School District dissolved and annexed to District # 6 on August 16, 1954.

District #6 would be annexed to Dixon District #170 in 1956.

Hill School, District #06

Hill School was located on the corner of Rock Island and Hoyle Roads in Nelson Township.

Hill School District became part of Dixon District #170 on July 16, 1956.

Hill school would operate as an attendance center for District #170 until it closed in 1958.

Hill School 1956

King School, District #10

King School was located on the northeast corner of Route 30 and Harmon Road in Nelson Township.

King School 1956

King District was known as District #9 and included the old schools of Union Harmon and Nelson prior to being District #10. (Source: Illinois Historical Society, January 1918 Issue)

King School District became part of Dixon District #170 on July 16, 1956. King School would operate as an attendance center for District #170 until it closed in 1958.

Nelson School, District #08

Nelson School is located on Pope Street in the Village of Nelson, in Nelson Township.

Nelson Elementary School, District #08 2006

In 1922 a new brick school was built in Nelson. In 1960, an addition was added which included a gymnasium and two classrooms.

Nelson School District is now a K-8 elementary district. The high school students attend school in Rock Falls, IL.

Walker School, District #09

Walker School was located on the corner of Atkinson and Walker Roads in Nelson Township.

Walker School District became part of Dixon District #170 on July 16, 1956. Walker school would operate as an attendance center for District #170 until it closed in 1958.

In 1976 a new home was being sought for the school after the building was donated to the Lee County Bicentennial Commission. (Rockford Newspaper, March 3, 1976) The fate of the school is not known.

The above photo taken was taken in 1956.

Sixteen

Palmyra Township

Gap Grove School, District #04

Gap Grove School was located on the northeast corner of Lenox and Prairieville Roads in Palmyra Township.

Gap Grove School dissolved on July 16, 1956 and became part of Dixon District #170.

The school operated as an attendance center for District #170 until it closed in about 1957.

Mound School, District #01

Mound School was located on the southeast corner of Penrose and Mound Hill Roads in Palmyra Township.

Mound School dissolved on July 16, 1956. The non-high school portion annexed to Dixon District #170. The portion in Sterling Township High School District #300 annexed to Jordan Elementary School District #143.

Mound School 1956

Oak Forest School, District #05

Oak Forest School was located on Route 2, east of Plock Road, on the north side of the road in Palmyra Township.

Oak Forest School dissolved on July 16, 1956 and became part of Dixon District #170.

Oak Forest School operated as an attendance center until it closed in 1958.

Oak Forest School as it looked in the 1950's

Prairieville School (Built 1858), District #200

Prairieville School was located in the village of Prairieville in Palmyra Township. The first schools around Prairieville were held in log cabins, a barn, and inside homes. A building for the sole purpose of a school was built in the 1850's. This was a brick building and was known as Grott School. Grott School closed in 1858 and was sold at auction. It was converted into a dwelling and finally demolished in 1917.

In 1858 a two story brick school was built in Prairieville at a cost of $3000. At the time the building was unmatched by any building in the area and gave the Prairieville area recognition of a progressive community.

The school would be the center of most local events. One interesting event was the celebration of the pavement between Sterling and Dixon being completed on the Lincoln Highway in 1920.

Just after midnight on January 17, 1930 a motorist passing on the Lincoln Highway noticed that the school was on fire. Early arrivers at the fire were able to save items such as the piano, pictures, books, and other items but the building would be gutted by the fire. The next day the standing brick walls were pulled down to prevent accidents on the property. School would be held in the Prairieville Church. On January 29, 1930 the board and insurance company agreed that the total of $5750 would be paid for the loss of the school and contents. By the second week of February 1930, the site was cleaned up and plans were under way to replace the school. (Source: History of the Prairieville School. 1850 – 1950)

Prairieville School (Built 1930), District #200

On January 17, 1930 the old Prairieville School burned down. A passing motorist saw the flames and with the exception of a few items that were saved, the school was a total loss. By the end of January the insurance was decided and by the second week of February the site was cleared of the remaining debris.

On February 25 the voters of the district approved the building of a new school on the same site as the old. The vote was unanimously approved 46-0. A second vote to approve bonds was approved for the construction of a new school. Bids were taken but the amounts were more then expected. Changes were made to the specifications and Henry Mades of Polo IL was awarded the contract. On May 19th construction started on the school. Area men donated time and trucks to haul 25000 bricks from Dixon to the construction site. It took a total of 35 truck loads over 1 ½ days to complete the task.

Buried beneath the cornerstone of the school is a copper box that contains items such as the history of the school, photographs, a map of District #200, copies of both the Dixon Telegraph and Sterling Gazette, coins, and other items.

Although the interior was not yet completed, the school was dedicated on September 1, 1930. It would continue to serve the people of Prairieville as a school for over the next forty years. Prairieville School became part of Sterling Community Unit District #5 in Whiteside County on July 1, 1972. (Source: History of the Prairieville School. 1850 – 1950)

Sugar Grove School (Built 1883), District #02

Sugar Grove School was located at the junction of Sugar Grove, Peek Home, and Timber Creek Roads in Palmyra Township. The original Sugar Grove Church and School was first built in 1846 by Jesse Seavey. That building was small and was replaced in 1857. In about the same spot a brick school/church combination was built. Later the building was condemned and replaced with a frame building that burned down in February of 1883. The school pictured above was built in 1883 and was completed in time for students to attend that fall. The building served multiple purposes including non denominational church meetings over the years.

Sugar Grove School District dissolved on July 16, 1956 and became part of Dixon District #170. The school remained open and operated as an attendance center for Dixon District #170 until it closed about 1958. At the time of the closing of Sugar Grove School about 20 to 25 students were attending classes there. Although about sixteen families petitioned the change the school board approved the closing and the students were to attend Jefferson School in Dixon the fall of 1958. (Dixon Telegraph, 1958)

Sugar Grove School would be abandoned for the next 22 years. During that time it suffered from repeated vandalism. The walls and roof were damaged by water and years of general decay. In 1980 a group of local residents met and decided to form the Sugar Grove Restoration Committee. Over the next several years they renovated the building and it is now open to the community for meetings, reunions, and other gatherings. (Dixon Telegraph)

Wild Cat School, District #03

Wild Cat School was located on Wild Cat Road, south of Timber Creek Road, on the south side of the road in Palmyra Township.

Wild Cat School dissolved and on July 16, 1956 and became part of Dixon District #170. The school operated as an attendance center until it closed about 1957.

Wolverine School, District #163

Wolverine School was located on Wolverine Road, north of Route 2, on the west side of the road in Palmyra Township.

Wolverine School dissolved and on July 16, 1956 and became part of Dixon District #170.

Wolverine School operated as an attendance center for District #170 until it closed in about 1958.

Wolverine School 1956

Seventeen
Reynolds Township

Brush Grove School, District #210

Brush Grove School was located on Brush Grove Road, south of Gurler Road, on the east side of the road in Reynolds Township.

Brush Grove School District became part of Rochelle Consolidated District #231 in 1948.

Brush Grove School was also known as Menz School.

Gooch School, District #110

Gooch School was located on the northeast corner of Elva and Brooklyn Roads in Reynolds Township.

Gooch School District became part of Community Unit District #271 on July 1, 1948. The school closed in 1949.

Hawkins School also known as Kersten School, District #111

Hawkins School was located on the northwest corner of Concord Road and Route 251 in Reynolds Township.

Part of Hawkins School District became part of Community Unit District #271 and part became part of Rochelle Community District #231 on July 1, 1948. Hawkins School closed in 1949.

Hawkins School was also known as Kersten School.

Miller School, District #115

Miller School was located on the southwest corner of McGirr and Melugins Grove Road in Reynolds Township.

Miller School District became part of Community Unit District #271 on July 1, 1948. The school closed in 1949.

Salzman School, District #116

Salzman School was located on the northeast corner of Herman and Brooklyn Roads in Reynolds Township.

Salzman School District became part of Community Unit District #271 on July 1, 1948. The school closed in 1949.

Stone Ridge School, District #114

Stone Ridge School was located on Rochelle Road, north of Reynolds Road, on the west side of the road in Reynolds Township.

Stone Ridge School District became part of Community Unit District #271 on July 1, 1948. The school closed in 1949.

Sullivan School, District #112

Sullivan School was located on the southwest corner of Elva and Melugins Grove Roads in Reynolds Township.

Sullivan School District closed in 1944 and became part of Community Unit District #271 on July 1, 1948.

Weiner School, District #113

Weiner School was located on McGirr Road, east of Brooklyn Road, on the south side of the road in Reynolds Township.

Weiner School District became part of Community Unit District #271 on July 1, 1948. Weiner School closed and became part of Ashton District #275 on March 19, 1956.

Eighteen
South Dixon Township

Red Brick School, District #32

Red Brick School was located on the southeast corner of Route 52 and Red Brick Road in South Dixon Township.

The school was originally located across the road and was known as Edson School. Later it was known as the St. James School and finally, The Red Brick School. On November 25, 1859 the township trustees bought land for the purpose of building a school. It was known as being one of the more progressive schools in the county. The school was one of the first to have a piano and its own well. (Source: 1954 Amboy Elementary Yearbook)

Red Brick School District became part of Amboy Community Unit District #272 on July 1, 1949. The school continued to stay open as an attendance center for District #272. In 1957 the Red Brick School closed and the students started attending school at the new attendance center in Eldena.

Ortgiesen School also known as Duis School, District #34

Ortgiesen or Duis School was located on Dutch Road, south of Renner Road, on the east side of the road in South Dixon Township.

The school district dissolved by action of Township Trustees in 1951.

Eldena School, District #36

Eldena School was located on the northeast corner of South Eldena and Eldena Roads in South Dixon Township.

Eldena School District became part of Amboy Community Unit District #272 on July 1, 1949. In 1957 a new school was built in Eldena.

Kelly School, District #33

Kelly School was located on the southwest corner of Hanne and Pump Factory Roads in South Dixon Township.

Kelly School District closed in 1947 and in 1951 the district was dissolved by action of the Township Trustees.

Lievan School, District #31

Lievan School was located on the northeast corner of Lievan and Pump Factory Road in South Dixon Township.

Lievan School District became part of Dixon District #170 on July 16, 1956.

Lievan School operated as an attendance center for District #170 until it closed in 1958.

Lievan School 1956

Will School also knows as Meese School, District #35

Will School was located on Route 26, near South Eldena Road, on the west side of the road in South Dixon Township.

Will School District closed in 1947 and dissolved by action of the Township Trustees in 1951.

Will School was also known as Meese School.

Preston School, District #29

Preston School was located on Route 2, north of Lievan Road, on the east side of the road in South Dixon Township.

Preston School District dissolved and became part of Dixon District #170 on July 16, 1956.

Preston School operated as an attendance center for District #170 until it closed in 1958.

Preston School 1956

White Temple School, District #30

White Temple School was located on the southwest corner of Route 52 and Eldena Road in South Dixon Township.

White Temple School District dissolved and became part of Dixon District #170 on July 16, 1956.

White Temple School operated as an attendance center for District #170 until it closed in 1958

White Temple School 1956

Nineteen
Sublette Township

Angier School, District #106

Angier School was located on St. Mary's Road, east of Green Wing Road, on the south side of the road in Sublette Township.

Angier School District closed in 1946 and the students started attending school at Sublette, District #103. (Sublette Centennial, 1847 - 1957) Sublette District #103 became part of Amboy Community Unit District #272 on July 1, 1949.

On July 8, 1950 District #272 auctioned off Angier School. The school was purchased by Elizabeth Angier for $137.50. (Amboy News, July 13 1950)

Austin School, District #104

Austin School was located on the southwest corner of Maytown and Green Wing Roads in Sublette Township.

Austin School District closed in 1922 and the students would attend school at Sublette, District #103. (Sublette Centennial, 1847 - 1957) Sublette, District #103 became part of Amboy Community Unit District #272 on July 1, 1949.

On July 8, 1950 District #272 auctioned off Austin School. The school was purchased by George Vaessen for $625. (Amboy News, July 13 1950)

Bartlett School, District #108

Bartlett School was located on the southeast corner of Todd and Wolf Roads in Sublette Township.

Bartlett School District closed in 1941 and the students attended Sublette, District #103 Sublette. (Source: Sublette Centennial, 1847 - 1957)

District #103 became part of Amboy Community Unit District #272 on July 1, 1949.

Clink School, District #102

Clink School was located on Tower Road, west of Slant Road, on the north side of the road in Sublette Township.

Clink School District closed in 1934 and the students attended school in Sublette, District #103. (Source: Sublette Centennial, 1847 - 1957)

Sublette District #103 became part of Amboy Community Unit District #272 on July 1, 1949.

Ellsworth School, District #105

Ellsworth School was located on the southwest corner of Route 52 and Maytown Road in Sublette Township.

Ellsworth School District closed in 1945 and the students attended school in Sublette, District #103 (Source: Sublette Centennial, 1847 - 1957).

Sublette became part of Amboy Community Unit District #272 on July 1, 1949.

Gentry School, District #100

Gentry School was located on the southwest corner of Route 52 and Green Wing Road in Sublette Township.

Gentry School District closed in 1939 and the students attended school at Sublette, District #103. (Source: Sublette Centennial, 1847 - 1957)

Sublette, District #103 became part of Amboy Community Unit District #272 on July 1, 1949.

Henkel School, District #109

Henkel School was located on Henkel Road, west of Route 52, on the north side of the road in Sublette Township.

Henkel School District closed in 1942 and the students attended school at Sublette, District #103. (Source: Sublette Centennial, 1847 - 1957)

Henkel School District became part of Mendota Community Consolidated District #289 in 1950.

Hubbell School also known as Reis School, District #107

Hubbell School was located on Center Road, south of St. Mary's Road, on the west side of the road in Sublette Township.

Hubbell School District closed in 1942. After 1942 the students from Hubbell School would attend school in Sublette, District #103. (Source: Sublette Centennial, 1847 - 1957)

The Sublette District became part of Amboy Community Unit District #272 on July 1, 1949. Hubbell School was also known as Reis School.

Sublette School, District #103

Sublette School was located on Sublette Road, East of Route 52, on the south side of the road, in the Village of Sublette, in Sublette Township. Early schools in Sublette, as with other Lee County schools, started out in a variety of places such as within churches, empty farm buildings, and log buildings. In 1861 land was purchased from the Illinois Central Rail Road, for the purpose of building a school. The school in Sublette would absorb many of the one room school houses throughout Sublette Township as they closed over the years. The school would switch from a one room school to a two room school depending on the enrollment. Sublette School District became part of Amboy Community Unit District #272 on July 1, 1949. Sublette continued to stay open as an attendance center for District #272 but was suffering from overcrowding in the old school.

In 1955 the voters voted to construct four new buildings with one being erected in Sublette. Construction for the new school would start in 1956 and the new four room school would open in September of 1957. (Source: Sublette Centennial, 1847 - 1957)

Sublette School. 1957

Theiss School, District #101

Thiess School was located on the southwest corner of Center and Tower Road in Sublette Township.

Theiss School District became part of Amboy Community Unit District #272 on July 1, 1949.

St. Mary's School, Sublette

The original St. Mary's school in Sublette opened in 1876. It was described as a one room clap board building with log ceilings and floors. Next to the school was a stable for those who rode their horses to school. The school supplied the water for the horses but the students were responsible for their feed.

In 1913 construction on a new brick building was started and completed in 1914. The first graduating class from the new brick school was in 1915. About 1959 Father Edward Lehman decided that the school needed remodeling. Some of the changes were that a kitchen was installed in the basement and the main

entrance was moved so that it faced the church. The architect for the project was John McLane Company. The attendance of the school started to decline shortly after the remodeling. The railroad left Sublette and the population started to decline, forcing the school to close in 1967. The building was eventually torn down in 2003. (Source, Peggy Armstrong)

After the 1959 remodeling

Twenty
Viola Township

Dunton School, District #117

Dunton School was located on the northwest corner of Lee and Town Hall Roads in Viola Township.

Dunton School District became part of Community Unit District #271 on July 1, 1948. Dunton School closed in 1949.

Bernardin School, District #120

Bernardin School was located on the southwest corner of Route 30 and Town Hall Road in Viola Township.

Bernardin School Bernardin School District closed and became part of Community Unit District #271 on July 1, 1948.

Bernardin School in about 1904. The above photo was of poor quality.

To the Right is an inside look at the school after a new building was erected.

Adrian School, District #123

Adrian School was located on Fisk Road, north of Beemerville Road, on the west side of the road in Viola Township.

Adrian School District closed in 1943 and became part of Community Unit District #271 on July 1, 1948.

The photo above shows the inside of the new building. The photo to the right was of the old school and taken in 1904.

Ross School, District #119

Ross School was located on the northeast corner of Butler and Brooklyn Roads in Viola Township.

Ross School District closed in 1933 and became part of Community Unit District #271 on July 1, 1948.

Fairview School, District #164

Fairview School was located on the northeast corner of Nichols and Brooklyn Roads in Viola Township.

Fairview School District closed in 1936 and became part of Community Unit District #271 on July 1, 1948.

Unfortunately some of the photos could not be located. Fairview School is one of those schools.

Van Campen School (Built 1906), District #122

Van Campen School was located on the northwest corner of Butler Hill and Melugins Grove Roads in Viola Township.

Van Campen School District became part of Community Unit District #271 on July 1, 1948. The school closed in 1950.

Original Van Campen School

In 1904 the Superintendent of Schools, Isaac F. Edwards, had pictures taken of all the Lee County Schools. Due to the condition of the Van Campen School it was decided to have a school rebuilt. The estimated cost was $1000. (Source: 1904 Newspaper Clipping, Publisher Unknown)

Van Petten School, District #118

Van Petten School was located on Lee Road, east of Route 251, on the north side of the road in Viola Township.

Van Petten School District closed and became part of Community Unit District #271 on July 1, 1948.

Webber School, District #121

Webber School was located on Route 30, east of Fisk Road, on the north side of the road in Viola Township.

Webber School District became part of Community Unit District #271 on July 1, 1948. The school closed in 1953.

Twenty One
Willow Creek Township

Byrd School, District #141

Byrd School was located on Lee Road, west of Paw Paw Road, in Willow Creek Township.

Byrd School closed in 1947 and the district became part of Community District #271 on July 1, 1948.

Hilleson School, District #143

Hilleson School was located on the northeast corner of Route 30 and Woodlawn Road in Willow Creek Township.

Hilleson School District became part of Community District #271 on July 1, 1948. In 1949 Hilleson School District became part of Community District #425 in Dekalb County. Hilleson School closed in 1949. The students probably attended school in Lee IL. (Lee IL, Then and Now 1874 – 1974)

Howlett School, District #154

Howlett School was located on the northeast corner of Howlett and Woodlawn Roads in Willow Creek Township.

On July 27, 1894 James C. Howlett and wife deeded to the trustees of schools the land that Howlett School was on. The deed stated, "This land is sold for a site for public school house: when it ceases to be used for such purpose then it shall revert to the grantor herein or to his heirs, executors, administrators or assigns." (Lee/Ogle Regional Office of Education records)

Howlett School District became part of Community District #271 on July 1, 1948. Howlett School closed in 1947.

Prior to Howlett School the school was known as the Allen Grove School.

Lee School, District #165

Lee School was located in the Village of Lee, in Willow Creek Township. During the early years of Lee there were several different schools including those in homes and those that served multiple purposes. In 1878 a building was built for the sole purpose of holding school. In 1890 a larger building was erected (Pictured Above) that included an elementary school and a two year high school. The school would later meet the state requirements to become a three year high school. In 1936 a new school opened in Lee (Picture Below) and the old building was sold at auction in May, 1940. In 1961 an addition was put on. Lee District #165 became part of Unit District #425 in 1949 (Now Indian Creek District #425). Lee School operated as an elementary school and the high school students attended school in Shabbona. Later all students would eventually attend schools in Shabbona. (Lee, IL - Then and Now, 1874 - 1974)

Lee School, As an apartment building in 2006

Miller School, District #144

Miller School was located on Stambrook Road, west of Steward Road, on the south side of the road in Willow Creek Township.

Miller School District closed and became part of Community District #271 on July 1, 1948.

Moffatt School, District #145

Moffatt School was located on Paw Paw Road, North of Howlett Road, on the west side of the road in Willow Creek Township.

Moffat School District became part of Community District #271 on July 1, 1948. Moffatt School closed in 1955.

Risetter School, District #142

Risetter School was located on the southwest corner of Route 30 and Paw Paw Road in Willow Creek Township.

Risetter School District became part of Community District #271 on July 1, 1948. In 1949 Risetter School District became part of Community Unit District #425 in Dekalb County. Risetter School Closed in 1949.

Risetter may have also been known as Townhouse School. (Lee/Ogle Regional Office of Education records)

Scarboro School (Built 1911), District #140

Scarboro School was located on Steward Road, north of Creek Road, on the west side of the road in Willow Creek Township.

In the 1850's the school was known as Twin Groves School. (Lee/Ogle Regional Office of Education records) The original school building was built in 1852. That building was sold at an auction in about 1857 for $125. The money from the sale was used to build a new building which burned in 1869. Within one week of the fire, the directors of the school made plans for a new school to be built. The contract for the new school called for a building 18 x 24 feet with a two foot stone foundation. Window sills were to be made of pine and minimum sizes were specified. The school was to seat 20 with patent iron standers, six windows, one door, a chimney, venetian blinds, and two coats of green paint. The work was to be completed by June 1 with the estimated cost set at $625. The new school was built across the road from where the old school stood. (Dixon Evening Telegraph, February 28, 1976)

The pictured building was built in 1911 at a cost of $2000 and was considered one of the best in Illinois at the time. The school had a library that was considered a gem and was stocked with books that a school would need for that time. The school had two ward rooms and lighting was considered to be excellent. (Dixon Weekly Citizen, May 22, 1913)

Scarboro School District became part of Community District #271 on July 1, 1948. On June 27, 1956 Scarboro was detached from District #271 and annexed to Shabbona District #425. The school was closed in 1956.

Twenty Two
Wyoming Township

Beemerville School, District #146

Beemerville School was located on Beemerville Road, West of Bingham Road, on the south side of the road in Wyoming Township.

The school was named after Jesse J. Beemer Sr. who donated the land on which the school was built. He made a provision that if the school closed, the land would return to his heirs. (Lee/Ogle Regional Office of Education records)

Beemerville School became part of Community Unit District #271 on July 1, 1948. Beemerville School closed about 1949.

Cottage Hill School, District #151

Cottage Hill School was located on the southwest corner of Cottage Hill and Angling Roads in Wyoming Township.

Cottage Hill School became part of Community Unit District #271 on July 1, 1948. Cottage Hill School closed in 1952.

Cyclone School, District #153

Cyclone School was located on the southwest corner of Cyclone and Earlville Roads in Wyoming Township.

Cyclone School became part of Community Unit District #271 on July 1, 1948. Cyclone School closed about 1953.

According to an article written by Mary Politsch the original school was destroyed by a cyclone on June 27, 1890, thus the name Cyclone School was given to the new school. (Lee/Ogle Regional Office of Education records)

Bridge School, District #152

Bridge School was located in Wyoming Township.

Mary Politsch was asked to write about her memories of Bridge School. She recalled that it was old and not well cared for. The school had a poor heating setup and corn and coal were stored inside the building for the stove. Water was carried to the school from a local farm. The average attendance at any one time was about eight to nine students. She recalled the school being located South of Paw Paw, just west of the bridge by the railroad tracks. She thought that the school was burned down by tramps from along the railroad. (Source: Paw Paw 1882 – 1982 Centennial Booklet)

The school closed in 1916 and in 1926 was added to Cyclone School District #153.

Jonesville School, District #147

Jonesville School was located on the northeast corner of Chicago and German Roads in Wyoming Township.

Jonesville School became part of Community Unit District #271 on July 1, 1948. Jonesville School closed about 1955.

Paw Paw School (1885 Building), District #149

Paw Paw Schools were located in Paw Paw, in Wyoming Township. During the early years Paw Paw had several schools. The following information was gathered from the 1902 Paw Paw Yearbook which was called The Cue.

In 1848 a building on the west side of Peru Street was used as a school. The students sat on slab benches and had no desks. That building was converted into a dwelling and in 1850 a new school building was erected. That building was later converted into a home sometime before 1902. (The Cue)

Another building was built sometime before 1882. In 1882 it was decided to enlarge the school. The addition gave the school a peculiar look and the school became known as the Camel's-Back School House. This schoolhouse burned in 1884 and was replaced in 1885. (The Cue)

In 1885 a new four room brick building replaced the Camel's Back School House. School would continue here until January 1897 when this school would also burn. Classes were held in the Methodist Church and another building on the main street. (The Cue)

Paw Paw School (1897 Building), District #149

A vote was taken to move the location for the new school that was to be built. In October of 1897 a new school was completed. Since it was not completed until October school did not commence until then. The new school had six classrooms, two large corridors, a library, a small laboratory on the upper floors, and a larger laboratory and play-room in the basement. In 1900 the school would become an accredited twelve year school recognized by the higher institutions such as Illinois University. (The Cue) It was probably about this time that the High School District #253 was formed. In 1924 the building received extensive remodeling and just about one year later on November 17, 1925 the building was gutted by fire. High School would be held at the Presbyterian Church and the Odd Fellows Hall. Grade School classes were held at the Methodist Church. (Lee/Ogle Regional Office of Education records)

Paw Paw School, Photo from 1922 Paw Paw Yearbook

Paw Paw School, District #149 and #253

The above Paw Paw school building was completed in 1926. Paw Paw Schools became part of Community Unit District #271 on July 1, 1948.

In 1948 and 1950 two additional buildings were moved to the school grounds to accommodate students who arrived after the closing of many rural schools. (Lee/Ogle Regional Office of Education records) The school was one of the very first to have a gymnasium. In addition to the gymnasium the school had six rooms and a corridor on the top floor, five rooms and a larger room on the first floor, and five rooms and the gymnasium in the basement. An addition was added in 1968 that included another gymnasium. This building would serve both the elementary and high schools until a new building would be built in 1958 for the high school. In 1958 it was decided that the school needed to be remodeled to better serve the grade school students. Work was started in 1959 and completed in 1960. (Source: Paw Paw Library)

Paw Paw High School, District #171

Paw Paw High School was built in 1958 to house the high school students and to alleviate overcrowding in the present building. (Source: Lee/Ogle Regional Office of Education records) The building contained nineteen rooms, a cafeteria, and a gymnasium. District #171 included the schools in Franklin Grove until 2004 when Franklin Grove detached and became part of Ashton/Franklin Center District #250. (Source: Lee/Ogle Regional Office of Education records) The above picture is from the 1971 Paw Paw School Year Book.

Paw Paw Elementary School, District #171

In about 2000 an addition was added to the existing high school for use by the elementary students of Paw Paw. The picture above shows the addition as it looks in 2006.

Radley School, District #150

Radley School was located near Paw Paw, in Wyoming Township.

Radley School closed and became part of Community Unit District #271 on July 1, 1948. Radley was also known as Ralley School.

Earlier Photo of Radley School

South Paw Paw School, District #161

South Paw Paw School was located on Paw Paw Road, just north of the Dekalb County Line, in Wyoming Township.

South Paw Paw School became part of Community Unit District #271 on July 1, 1948. South Paw Paw School closed in 1949.

East Paw Paw School, District #162

East Paw Paw School was located in Wyoming Township.

A building was built in 1855 as a seminary but was later sold to the school district. In 1968 the seminary reopened and was known as the East Paw Paw Teacher's Institute and Classical Seminary. In 1870 that building burned and the building built in 1855 was turned over to the seminary and school continued there. (Source: Paw Paw Library)

Twenty Three
Other Schools

Riverside School, District #207

Riverside School was located just across the Lee County line in Ogle County.

According to the 1935 Lee County Plat Map a large portion of District #207 was located in Lee County just east of Grand Detour, across the Rock River.

Index of Schools

Acknowledgements

I truly appreciate all of the support from those who shared stories and pictures for this book. This list of individuals is to numerous to mention and to avoid missing some names I won't try to list them all. I do appreciate my wife, Jodie, for her patience during the several months that I spent working on this project.

I wish to thank the following organizations and their employees and/or volunteers who were of great help: The Lee/Ogle Regional Office of Education; The Loveland Community Building; The Franklin Grove Public Library; The Mills & Petrie Memorial Library; The Paw Paw Public Library; Dixon Public Schools, and the Amboy Depot Museum. Special thanks to the Lee County Genealogical Society for their support with this project. Without them I would not have been able to accomplish this task.

www.ingramcontent.com/pod-product-compliance
Lightning Source LLC
Chambersburg PA
CBHW030926090426
42737CB00007B/339